IN THE CREATIVE ARENA

Why Creativity Is Key To Building Your Future

Tony Albrecht

Offscripting Press

ISBN: 978-1-7356058-2-1

To Wylder and Sky,

Write your own stories out here.

Write them big.

Write them true.

Write them as only you can.

INTRODUCING

While in high school, I wrote a short story that was then printed in *Sisyphus*, the school literary journal. The story's title was "Freezing in Chicago," and it was about a kid affected by seeing a homeless guy on the street during a Christmas shopping trip to Chicago.

When I ran into Rich Moran, my English teacher sophomore year, thirteen years later in a coffee shop in St. Louis, he remembered "Freezing in Chicago." Even brought the story up by name.

I tell you that little story because, as I'm typing these words, that remains the pinnacle of my literary career. I had ambitions to write for a living, majoring in English Composition and writing columns for the *Index*, Truman State University's weekly newspaper. But by the time I graduated with a BA, I couldn't do it.

Sure, I could write technically effective and elegant prose, but I couldn't open myself to criticism. My ego couldn't handle so much as the possibility that people might not like what I wrote.

So I stopped writing, opting to try law school instead. Becoming a lawyer offered the safe, comfortable course, an unassailable professional trajectory, and most certain success.

As we'll get into, that decision had consequences, and I now see those consequences as a direct result of turning away from my creative impulses. Conversely, my life began improving when I once again embraced my creativity and started exercising those muscles again. I am now, twelve days shy of my fortieth birthday, living what I would describe as a creative life.

Part of my creative process involves relentless and frequent iteration. This page is a perfect example. The first page you're reading is the last page I'm writing, and my editor will see it for the first time only when she receives her signed copy. I'm sending the final manuscript of this book off for formatting today.

I've also learned to share the things I make, whether blogs, businesses, or this book. With any luck, I'll have an obvious new literary pinnacle upon releasing this thing into the world.

Will I become a best-selling author? Probably not.

But I *am* a bona fide Creative Contender. Through more trial and error than I'd care to admit, I've learned how to take an idea and put in the Work necessary to turn it into a shipped project. The twenty-three-year-old version of me couldn't ship work, so he never had a prayer of succeeding as a creative. Now that I'm older and at least less scared, if not wiser, I know that the only shot at creative success depends on the willingness to step into the Creative Arena and let it rip.

Steven Pressfield's *The War of Art* is my creativity holy book. This book you're reading might be nothing more than a half-baked homage to that one. In *The War of Art*, Pressfield relays a story about the first professional writing job he ever got, as a screenwriter for a King Kong movie that bombed. Pressfield said he was crushed by the failure. In his forties, divorced, and having sacrificed dearly for his craft, he felt worthless and washed up. Until a friend asked if he was going to quit.

The answer to that, of course, was hell no.

"Then be happy," the friend replied. "You're where you wanted to be, aren't you? So you're taking a few blows. That's the price for being in the arena and not on the sidelines."

Pressfield realized then that although he had not yet had success as a writer, he had just had his first real failure.

This little book hopes to inspire you.

If you're currently living on the sidelines, it's time to enter the Creative Arena. If you're already in there, taking swings and taking punches, let's commiserate.

Because no matter how many times we get knocked down, once we've tasted that thrill of being in the arena . . . retreating to the sidelines isn't really an option, is it?

All right, let's go.

TWO SELVES

I have two versions of me inside. Two Tonys, if you will. They're not friends and not quite enemies, though they don't like each other. They're like siblings who have a certain affinity for each other but can't get along. That's mainly due, I believe, to the fact that the two Tonys are locked in a perpetual struggle for domination of my life, and if one is winning a given day, the other must necessarily be losing.

One Tony is the Creative Couch Potato.

The other Tony wants to be a Creative Contender.

While writing is the medium I use most often when describing how creativity manifests in my life, the two Tonys wrestle over far more than typing words on the page. Their daily struggle largely determines the course of my life, at least when it comes to the decisions I make about things I can control.

They fight over:

- Whether to exercise;
- How many cookies I'm going to eat today;
- Which career path to take;
- How to spend enough time my wife and kids;
- How much time to spend away from my phone;
- Which creative projects to start; and, of course,
- Whether to bother with finishing and shipping projects I've started.

In short, they wrestle about anything and everything that has implications for the quality of my life. And they have very different ideas of what my life should look like.

Couch Potato Tony likes to be comfortable. He likes easy, convenient. He will, without fail, choose the path of least resistance. He will find any excuse to not get off the couch and run . . . or sit down and write the 500 words . . . or have the challenging conversation . . . or put in the extra time on that work project . . . or eat the salad instead of the cheeseburger. Couch Potato Tony isn't a bad guy by any means. He's a great hang, fun to be around, loves jokes.

Creative Contender Tony, on the other hand, tends to be more serious.

He has big goals, dreams, aspirations, sh!t to do. He has a vision for what he wants life to look like one year or five years or ten years down the road. And he understands that whether he realizes that dream ten years from now depends in large part on the decisions he makes today. He, like Couch Potato Tony, enjoys a good time. He just prioritizes the big goals. Doing that results in a reverse engineering effect whereby he figures out what needs to be done today or this week to move toward achieving that big goal down the road. He needs discipline, timers, to-do lists, and calendars. He says no to a lot of invitations or puts himself in situations where he'll naturally get fewer invitations to begin with, which leaves him more bandwidth to focus on the big goals.

These are the two versions of myself slap-fighting between my ears every day. I'm guessing you've got something similar going on in your head, right?

Creative Couch Potato Tony, unfortunately, has had a winning record in daily wrestling matches since I was a teenager. He more or less won every day between the ages of twenty-two and twenty-eight, a solid six-year winning streak of more than two thousand matches.

Impressive.

Since 2010, though, when Creative Contender Tony decided to get up off the mat and start trying, he has proved a worthy opponent. By 2015, Contender Tony had the upper hand. As I write this in 2022, Contender Tony dominates Couch Potato Tony. The most recent estimates indicate that Contender Tony wins more than 75 percent of the matches.

How can I tell which Tony is winning?

Simple. I can take a look at how my life is going.

When Couch Potato Tony is having his way, I start to become physically unhealthy. I put on weight. I become more sedentary. My dietary choices go to hell. My binge watching goes way up. And, most notably, I more or less stop making creative Work. I become more of a passenger of my life, allowing events to carry me along, letting one day fade into the next without taking action to put my stamp on that day.

Couch Potato optimizes for comfort, and comfort is nice, but as Kahlil Gibran wrote in *The Prophet*, comfort is the thing that enters the house a guest, then becomes the host, and then the master.

To put it another way, if I don't watch it, I become my comfort zone's bitch. And that's not a good thing. Couch Potato Tony is a good hang, but I don't want him running my life.

Historically, change has come—or Contender Tony has started putting up more of a fight—once I notice just how much of a mess things are becoming. The most glaring example is the Guamanian jail story, the result of that six-year Couch Potato Tony winning streak.

Contender Tony had finally had enough. He was ready to see if he couldn't give Couch Potato Tony a run for his money.

And the results since 2010 have been encouraging based on what I've helped create.

- In 2013, I moved out of my apartment, quit my job, sold my car, and took a one-way ticket to Bangkok for what I expected to be a yearlong sabbatical from law. I intended to travel, volunteer, write, and generally gain a better sense of what I wanted to do with my life. That one year turned into four years between full-time roles and allowed me space to run a number of experiments, meet amazing people (including a beautiful Canadian who would become my wife), and see a lot of the world. I spent time in more than two dozen countries on four continents.
- In 2015, my sister Christie and I started a blog called

Offscripting. We had moderate success writing for a couple years about our respective decisions to pause our careers in search of a different way of life.

- The Offscripting Camino was a major offshoot of the blog. I was part of a team leading two groups of people on walking retreats along El Camino de Santiago, a pilgrimage route across a bit of France and northern Spain. One group walked 120 miles over ten days. The second group walked 500 miles over five weeks.

- In 2016, Christie and I started Artists Creating Supporting & Shipping (ACSAS), a support group for creativity. It was the precursor to what became the Rowdy Creative in 2022 and led to much of the thinking that has produced this book. Our primary accomplishment has been more than thirty cohorts of creatives learning to win the battle against Resistance and making progress on their personal projects, one day at a time.

- I married Sawil in 2016. We approached the wedding as an opportunity to exercise our creative muscles and create an unusual experience. We knew we wanted a small affair with relatively little stress, somewhere beautiful, preferably with mountains. Ultimately, we wanted an event that would allow our guests to focus on spending the time together. We opted for a weekend in the hills of Quebec, renting a couple large houses overlooking the St. Lawrence Seaway. It came off perfectly.

- In 2019, Sawil and I wanted to buy our first house together but fell ass-backward into having a house built in St. Louis, Missouri, instead. That part was fairly conventional. What became a creative act was what we did instead of putting a detached garage in the backyard (which is what just about every house had). We helped design a two-hundred-square-foot guesthouse in lieu of a garage. Our intention was to live in the house while also having it generate substantial income for our family. Plus, we'd spent so much time traveling and staying in hostels and Airbnbs that we wanted to try our hand with hospitality. So we opened St. Louis Tiny House, and it's become one of the city's highest-rated and most popular Airbnbs. We've been featured by the local STL paper and podcasts.

- I've been working on a book manuscript—not this one —since April 2020. *Only Drowning Men* is a peculiar memoir structured around emails exchanged between myself and Kevin Lamb, a close friend who died in 2018.
- There's a line I use regularly these days, and if you've messaged with me on LinkedIn, you might have already heard it. When Sawil agreed to move to St. Louis in 2017, she told me I had five years before I'd be going to Canada. Turns out, she meant it. In May 2021, we loaded our kids and some stuff into our Subaru and drove from St. Louis to Ontario, where we'd bought a house with eighteen acres of forest. We'd talked for years about wanting a slower pace of life for ourselves and for our kids. We also wanted to be closer to family. So we bought the place with Sawil's parents, converted the house into a two-family sort of affair, and converted an ATV garage on the property into the Writing Shed, a sweet little office lined with furniture-grade plywood. Sawil and I had both spent all our lives living in cities, so the change has been substantial. But a year into this experiment, we're grateful to have made the leap and are loving where we've landed.
- I've also conceived and produced some podcast episodes (eight) and YouTube videos (more than one hour). I'm no audio or video expert but have learned enough to be dangerous in both those mediums.

I share all those things about myself for a couple reasons. First, since I'm not a famous or known person at this point, there's no reason you'd know what my creativity has looked like in action.

Second, the case I'm making in this book ultimately isn't about doing more creative projects but about building a creative life, which is the product of executing a bunch of different creative projects.

After spending almost my entire twenties running away from my creativity, hiding from it, just wanting to be told what to do and receive rewards for jumping through hoops, I've spent the last twelve years on a fundamentally different trajectory —one where much of the time involves maneuvering beyond my comfort zone. The results have been more meaningful and fruitful than my scared, alcoholic self in 2009 could have possibly imagined.

A WHY-TO BOOK

This isn't a how-to book. It's a why-to book.

I'm making a case for why you should care about creativity —why you and I need to spend more time and energy developing our creative abilities.

At the heart of this book is the idea that you and I and everyone we know can become a Creative Contender, and putting in the time and effort to do that could be key to our future health, happiness, and success, both as humans and as professionals.

This isn't a long book, mainly because you don't need three hundred pages of a book about creativity by me. That said, I believe I can add something to the overall conversation about creativity happening in our culture right now.

We hear the word a lot.

Most of us like the idea.

We think we know it when we see it.

We want more of it.

But it seems that very few of us know:

1. What creativity actually is.
2. Why creativity matters.
3. Why so many of us became Creative Couch Potatoes unable to harness our creative powers.
4. How you can (and why you should) become a Creative Contender.

By the end of this book, I hope you'll have a better grasp of all four of those threads.

If you're heading in an uninspired direction, creativity might be the key to shifting directions and choosing a new trajectory—one that feels generative, full of possibilities, and all your own.

PART I

Creativity: The What and The Why

DICTIONARIES ON CREATIVITY

I was writing about creativity daily for some time before I realized that very few people—myself included, frankly—could clearly define the term. Then I started looking into it, beginning with the dictionary.

Merriam Webster, that most esteemed of wordsmiths, defines creativity as "the ability to create" or "the quality of being creative."

Not too helpful, right?

Then I checked Dictionary.com, that most Internetish of websites. Their contributions weren't much better. That site defines creativity as "the state or quality of being creative" or "the process by which one utilizes creative ability." To their credit, the folks at Dictionary.com do have a third definition consisting of twenty-six words that gets closer to something usable, though it's unclear how much of the improvement is simply a product of their having included so many words that at least a few were bound to be on the mark.

If the dictionaries can't figure out what creativity means, what hope do the rest of us have?

A USEFUL DEFINITION
OF CREATIVITY

Fortunately, there are a few people who have tried to unpack creativity in a more useful way. Sir Ken Robinson defined creativity as a system for generating new ideas that have value.

Teresa Amabile, a professor at the Harvard Business School, defines it as a process for generating ideas or problem solutions that are useful.

It's worth deconstructing those definitions a little bit to understand what exactly they're talking about.

First and foremost, we're talking about a process. Like baking a cake. The process of baking a cake requires having the right ingredients, combining them in the correct order, and baking the ingredients at the right temperature for the right amount of time. Collecting ideas and then turning them into finished products, projects, or performances also requires that we follow a process: the creative process.

Second, there's the matter of ideas: things produced by the imagination due to the brain connecting dots.

Third, we need some element of novelty or newness for a thing to be creative. The thing doesn't need to be the first of its kind, just new to you.

Fourth, to be creative, a new idea must also have some utility, which requires that an idea be put in motion. The thing can be tangible or intangible, but it must be a shipped thing. That doesn't mean it needs to be made public. Private works can still be creative works. Maybe the line is that it *could* be shared.

That said, I do believe that when ideas don't get shipped

as completed projects, they start to back up. Like plumbing. Unpleasant consequences might follow.

So creativity is a process, which means that in some sense there is *the* creative process, and it has component parts that are more or less universal regardless of the who, when, where, or what. We don't need to get overly complicated in describing what that process is. The creative process is about generating ideas, taking action to convert the idea to a thing, tangible or intangible, and then sharing it. Seth Godin uses the word *shipping* to describe the act of sharing creative work.

This book isn't about *the* creative process though. It's more about *your* creative process, because doing your Work with a capital W requires that you understand your process. The better we understand our processes as individuals, the better we can prepare ourselves for the daily wrestling match with Resistance. The more days we win that match, the more Work we make.

My hope with this book is that it can help you understand your process better. When, where, and how you Work the best. How you get your ideas. How you overcome the Dip, that inevitable valley Seth Godin has written about in a book of the same name. Understanding the process will make it easier for you to win your battle and to start stringing days (and Work) together.

YOUR PROCESS

Do you know what your creative process looks like?

Through most of my life, I couldn't have told you. I, like many of us, was (mis)led to believe that creativity is magical, the product of inspiration. It could not be predicted, only captured.

And, of course, there is something magical about creativity and the role that each of us plays in bringing new creations into the world. First, take how infinitesimal the odds were that you and I were ever born. Bake in our life's trajectories and experiences and interests. Add the things we encounter, see, notice. Then consider what we're capable of learning, doing, and making, and it all comes together to produce the potential for transforming new ideas into things.

Mason Currey wrote a book called *Daily Rituals*, recounting details from the creative processes of 160 creative people. From Freud to Austen, Hemingway to Beethoven. The main takeaway: how creative work gets done is a personal thing, and no two people do their Work the same way.

Flaubert didn't start his daily writing session on *Madame Bovary* until everyone else had gone to bed. Kafka was similar, wanting the quiet that could only be found late at night in the middle of Prague.

In *The War of Art*, Steven Pressfield describes his work as happening from about 9 a.m. until 1 p.m. Isaac Asimov, who published four hundred books during his life, wrote all the time. He started at 6 a.m. and wrote until 10 p.m., an ethic he attributed to working in his father's Brooklyn candy store from an early age. The candy store was open from 6 a.m. to 10 p.m., seven days a week, and Asimov adopted the same mindset when writing his books.

Toni Morrison, on the other hand, talked about how she had to work her writing around day jobs through most of her life. For a period, she might write early in the mornings, and then switch to writing in the late afternoons if she changed jobs and hours. Her routine produced a Nobel Prize.

I could go on, but the point is that to get really good at your creative process, you first need to understand:

a)   That you have one; and

b)   What it is.

Once you understand those things, you can start working to improve your process. That's what most of the rest of this book is about.

WHAT OF INSPIRATION?

The way we've described creativity so far, you might be under the impression that all creativity requires is a willingness to put your Butt in the Seat and work.

That's not right. Count me amongst those who believe that creativity has a mystical quality to it, something mysterious that involves, requires, and demands a willingness and ability to connect with some force that exists wholly beyond the realm between our ears. If I want to find inspiration, I can't try.

I have to get up and stop trying. I have to get busy doing something else, unbusy my mind as to the Work, and instead open up the possibility that the Muse, or inspiration, or the universe can whisper in my ear. I've heard inspiration described as a stream, and our job as creators is merely to come drink from the stream. I also like to think of inspiration as unseen but all around us in the air. All we need to do to be inspired is go out, look up, and breathe it in. Might take a minute or two, but if we're open to it, it'll happen.

Then there's the connection to other people. There is a myth about the lone creative genius. I don't know if the lone creative genius exists, but I know I'll never be that, and you most likely never will be either. Creativity is about connection, and that includes connecting with other people.

Is it a coincidence that so much amazing art was coming out of Florence during the Renaissance, out of Paris in the 1920s, from the Beatniks in the 1950s? No, it wasn't coincidence.

It was concentration. People who wanted to make stuff found themselves with other people serious about making stuff, resulting in a concentration of talent, energy, and ultimately, opportunity. In his book *Show Your Work!*, Austin Kleon talks about this idea as a scenius.

If you wanted to strengthen your physical muscles, you'd be best served by getting yourself to a gym every day. Become a gym rat. Make friends with the other gym rats. I've never been a gym rat and don't really like the gym, but I understand the appeal. I'm what you might call a trail-running rat. Some of my closest friends are also trail-running rats. Our relationship strengthens my desire to run trails, provides accountability for doing it, and gives me people to commiserate and celebrate with.

To get creatively fit, consider becoming a creativity rat. The Rowdy Creative is as good a place to start as any. We're a scenius, a group of creatives supporting one another on our journeys toward wherever it is we're going. All we know is that we're making more Work than we otherwise would and that the journey feels better when undertaken with friends.

A scenius also provides opportunities for cross-pollination. My sister Christie is a writer by trade and identity. But after watching a couple painters in our community do their thing, she decided to take up water colors. Turned out, she really enjoyed painting. She's not half-bad at it. And she's found that it helps with her writing, if only by getting the creative juices flowing, a product of making new connections.

Another benefit of a scenius is getting yourself an audience for your Work, particularly your earlier Work, before you have any audience and are doing your thing fueled by ambition and love of the game. There's a danger for creatives early in the journey that when your Work gets ignored—which will almost certainly happen—you mistakenly conclude that being ignored means the thing has no value, is no good. If it were any good, people would notice and the thing would take off. Right?

No.

Almost all of us are ignored when we start. Kevin Kelly

concocted an idea that we, as creatives, need one thousand true fans to make a living. I don't know if one thousand is the right number, but it's as good a number as any to shoot for. And my hunch is that the hardest fans to get are going to be Fan 1 through Fan 100. I think that's true for a couple reasons.

First, the bottom line is that you're most likely not that good when you start. Ira Glass of NPR fame has a brilliant bit about how we have a gap between our taste and our Work in the beginning. Our taste is killer, but our Work isn't that good. The hard part is sticking with the Work long enough to close the gap so that the Work getting made starts to live up to our (and other people's) standards. And during that time before we get some market validation or positive feedback that our Work doesn't suck, which might last years, we're far more likely to quit, shelve it for a while at least. If we're not making Work, then there's nothing for our potential fans to see and engage with. We have to keep making stuff for people to notice, even though they're not going to notice at first.

Which leads to the second point, which is that we human beings are drawn to like what other people like. Derek Sivers had a great TED Talk long ago about how it's actually the first follower who helps drive big ideas. The visionary, the one shouting about something new and exciting, is at risk of being just a crackpot—until people start enrolling to join that person on the journey. That first follower provides some level of proof that the idea has value. A second follower is far more likely to join once that first person is there to say, yeah, I know it sounds wild, but I think this person's onto something big.

Your scenius can be the group of people who both support you in putting one foot in front of the other while nobody is paying attention, and they can be your first followers, the first people to confirm to the public that you're worth paying attention to, you're a good one.

YOUR WORK

You likely have—or at least have had—a job or two. You've gone to work. You've worked. You know what work is.

But do you know what your Work is?

Put simply, your Work with a capital W is what you can do to make even the tiniest beautiful dent in the universe—that, if you don't do it, won't get done.

It's different than working. We're not talking about a vocation, though it could be. And it's probably not the job. We don't like to admit it, but when it comes to our jobs, most of us are far more replaceable than we'd like to think. Sure, it might be a pain in the ass to replace us, and maybe the replacement is only 95 percent as good at the job, but the enterprise will move forward. That show will go on without you.

Your Work, on the other hand, can only be done by you.

It is your book that only you can write.

It is your nonprofit organization that only you have envisioned.

It is your trip through Latin America that only you can undertake.

It is your business to help with the climate crisis that only you can start.

The reason your Work is up to you to do is that the motivation to do it comes from within. We are compelled to do this Work. In my experience, it tends to feel like I don't choose my Work—the Work chooses me.

Paradoxically, it is the uniqueness of the opportunity that is both what makes Work so compelling to us as individuals and also so difficult to pursue.

We are compelled by the possibility of doing, making, starting, or building something worthwhile, unique, impactful, interesting. We want to be a part of something worth being a part of.

But at the same time, if the thing were really all that worthwhile, then either somebody would already be doing it or somebody else far more talented and qualified *is* already doing it, and we just haven't heard about them yet. Either way, our efforts will be rendered futile because we're either wrong about the validity of the initial idea or will be outperformed by someone better.

That's Resistance talking. We're going to get into Resistance in some detail, but for the moment it suffices to say that getting creatively fit involves embracing the idea that you have Work to do, that pursuing your Work is worthwhile, and that you need to strengthen those creative muscles of yours because Resistance is going to show up every day to wrestle you in an attempt to keep you from doing that Work.

When I first heard the term Resistance, I immediately understood what it meant. It was Resistance that had landed me in a Guamanian jail cell.

MY CREATIVE
ROCK BOTTOM

On the morning after Thanksgiving of 2009, I regained consciousness on a concrete slab in a jail cell on the island of Guam. I was wearing a T-shirt, flip-flops, and basketball shorts from the eighth grade. The glaring fluorescents overhead stayed on all night.

Things weren't going well. I was very drunk, overweight, and lonely. Given that I'd just been arrested for (allegedly) driving under the influence, my career as a lawyer, which had begun only three months earlier, was already in jeopardy. Plus, if I didn't get out of that cell, I was going to be late for work.

Obviously, I had a number of things going on that led me to that Guamanian jail cell. But what I've come to believe is that I had let my creative muscles atrophy. I had let my creative ideas back up without the opportunity to become things in the real world. And not unlike a backed-up toilet, the result was a mess. What could have been my twenties spent writing or starting businesses, turned, by the time I was twenty-seven, into just wanting a templated life to follow.

I didn't want to create. I wanted to consume.

I didn't want to take chances. I wanted to be given opportunities.

Above all, I didn't want to fail. I was terrified of failure, of being discovered as a fraud. I wanted to succeed—not to feel the thrill of success so much as to avoid the feelings associated with not succeeding.

I had been a kid who loved to write. I had an active

imagination. I liked starting things. I wrote for the high school newspaper and had a short story published in the literary journal senior year. In college, I majored in English Composition, took creative writing classes, wrote columns for the weekly newspaper, and seriously considered pursuing a master in fine arts for creative writing.

In retrospect, it's clear that I probably should have considered entrepreneurship as a path, but I have no recollection of ever considering that possibility through college or law school. I don't know why entirely, but I thought in terms of career paths.

Being a lawyer meant one thing.

Being a writer meant another thing.

Being a public relations person meant something.

I thought in terms of paths to follow rather than trails to blaze.

By the time I was in law school, the most creative thing I did was organize a series of charity events with my buddy Brian. We conceived of the idea while studying in Berlin after our first year of law school. I'd underperformed and didn't have any great summer job prospects, so spending borrowed money to travel Europe seemed like as good a decision as any. I'd at least raise my GPA.

While drinking beers on a patio in Brussels over a weekend, we came up with an idea for a drinking games competition at our law school. Inspired by the movie *Beerfest*—if you haven't seen it, it's exactly what it sounds like—we conceived of a competition that, like the movie, would culminate in a final round relay race of drinking that required the anchor to chug from Das Boot, a giant glass stein in the shape of a boot. Inspired by the Manneken Pis, the famous fountain in Brussels of a little boy peeing, we called our thing the Potbelly Games.

We did indeed put on said event a few months later, and went on to host another as well as two trivia nights attended by hundreds. All in all, we raised more than $10,000 for charity.

Oh, and I also blew $1,500 at the last one by deciding to keep the open bar open one more hour at Humphrey's, the college bar where we hosted the after party.

That's the shadow at work.

The way I understand it now, the Potbelly Games were a shadow expression of my creativity. I'd turned away from being creative in favor of a safer path, so my creative impulses had to find ways out that my fear-driven little brain could accept. A drinking games competition for adults sufficed in its idiocy as to avoid detection as a truly creative act.

I went to my first meeting of Alcoholics Anonymous a week after waking up in that jail cell, and 2010 was a year of getting my head on straight, starting to regain some equilibrium mentally, spiritually, and physically. I heard that we hit rock bottom the moment we quit digging.

I stopped digging that night in 2009, both in terms of my drinking and also, as I now see it, in hiding from my creativity.

Sometimes I wonder what I might have produced during my twenties if I hadn't avoided my creative Work. Or hell, what I might have made in my thirties had I chosen to spend my twenties developing skills and pursuing curiosity rather than dulling my senses and carousing.

It doesn't matter. I'm not writing this book to tell you how great I am—or could have been—as a creative. No, my goal here is to offer myself as one example of an individual who ran into trouble by avoiding creativity in favor of mere productivity.

I know I am not alone. I know it's a problem for millions of other people.

The sooner we recognize the root of the problem and how it's affecting our careers and our lives, the sooner we can alter trajectories and start doing more of our Work.

BORN CREATIVE

Every once in a while, I find myself in a conversation with someone who says that kids aren't creative. And every time it happens, I'm newly annoyed at that specific person and astounded that anybody would have that opinion.

The author and scientist George Land ran a large study that began in 1968 and tracked creativity levels of children during the course of fifteen years. What he found was that five-year-old children achieved Genius Level at an incredible 98 percent clip. By the time kids were fifteen, though, the rate of creative geniuses had dropped to 12 percent. And by the time we're adults, only 2 percent of us could ace the thing.

Is what Land found accurate?

I'd encourage you to look into the study for yourself, though I'm including it here because it sets my argument up so very nicely.

My oldest child is almost four now, and he is a tornado of creative energy. Again, I'm defining creativity as a process for generating ideas that are new and valuable. My little man's synapses are firing off all day long, and he's always making new connections, the natural byproduct of having just gotten here and having very little idea how anything works.

He's constantly coming up with new stories, new songs, new games. It's worth noting he's not inventing stuff the world has never seen. But he is coming up with stuff that's new to him, which is the bar we're worried about. And as for the usefulness or value of what he makes, the enjoyment of the people around him—usually his parents or grandparents—suffices to clear that hurdle. The creativity has tremendous relational value, as he's learning how to relate to people while also strengthening bonds.

I'm resisting the urge to descend into a rabbit hole of stories about my son's creative impulses. While I believe that kids are born creative and think that matters, for purposes of this book, the point that really matters is one I expect we all can agree on:

We get less creative over time.

BUT ARE YOU CREATIVE?

The short answer:

Yes, you are a creative being.

Too many of us have confusion around this idea. It leads to our believing that we did not get any creativity when it was handed out in the beginning.

It seems like we get taught that creativity is something you either have or you don't, that it's like having red hair or being left-handed.

Do I have red hair?

No.

Am I left-handed?

You know it.

The answer is pretty clear cut, innate, unchangeable.

Creativity isn't like that. It's more like generosity. Catch me at any given moment, and I might be acting in ways that are not at all generous.

But I always have the potential to act generously. I can always be developing my generosity muscles. And if I do it enough, I might get so strong at being generous that people even start describing me that way.

Same goes for creativity. It's not something you are. It's something you do, develop, employ.

Use the muscle, and it gets stronger. Being creative gets easier. You can take on bigger creative challenges.

Don't use it, and it atrophies.

You might even end up thinking you aren't creative the

28

same way you don't have six toes on your right foot. If you are such a person, I feel you on that. And it's not your fault that you feel that way. It's not a failure on your part.

Let's talk for a minute about why so many of us made it to adulthood convinced we're just not creative at all.

A NATION OF WORKERS

I DON'T WANT A NATION OF THINKERS. I WANT A NATION OF
WORKERS.

— JOHN D. ROCKEFELLER

That quote from Rockefeller, one of the founding fathers of the American public education system, just about sums it up. He said that in 1900. Before cars. Before aviation. Before space flight. Before either World War. Before the United States transitioned from an industrial economy to an information economy. And obviously, before the Internet.

All that to say, a lot has changed since Rockefeller and whoever else was thinking about how to design an education system. In his famous TED Talk, Sir Ken Robinson lays out what our schools (the UK's system largely mirrors the American system) were primarily designed to teach.

We sat in rows. Raised our hands to go to the bathroom. Tried to produce the "right" answer on demand. Went through school in batches.

The schools designed in the early 1900s looked like factories because they were built to produce factory workers, people performing routine, repetitive tasks on assembly lines.

Rockefeller's quote above has aged rather poorly, hasn't it? But it made sense. As Seth Godin has written, our education system optimizes for obedience and compliance because that's what the Industrial Age required of us. The deal was that, if a person could show up on time, do the work competently, and not make a fuss, they could make a decent living. They could earn enough to provide for their families, buy a house and a car.

It wasn't necessarily a bad deal in terms of quality of life.

Or maybe it was. I'm not qualified to make that determination and don't have much interest in doing so. The point for our purposes is that, good or bad, that way of life no longer exists.

Which begs the question: why do we have the same school system as we did in the 1930s?

HOOP JUMPING

Frederick Taylor might be the most influential person you've never heard of in terms of the impact his work has had on your life. Taylor was a bean counter at a company called Bethlehem Steel, where he devised systems for people being more productive at work. He used stopwatches and measured inputs and outputs of productivity. His approach changed how factories and assembly lines operated.

His work led to how insanely efficient that Chick-fil-A drive-thru is (the guy sitting on the curb passing out sauces from a cart after the window seems a little extra, doesn't it?).

Taylor's work also contributed to how we go to school. Timed minimum proficiency exams are an example. A focus on finding a right answer is another.

By the time I graduated from high school in 2001, I had learned to avoid the red X on assignments. My goal on any given school assignment involved minimizing the amount of red ink on the page when I got it back.

The less red ink, the higher the grade on the assignment.

The higher the grade on the assignment, the higher the grade in the class.

The higher the grade in the class, the higher the GPA.

The higher the GPA, the higher rate of advanced classes.

The higher the rate of advanced classes, the better chance of getting into a "good" college.

The better chance of getting into a "good" college, the better chance of landing a great job.

Then, happiness and success all the way down.

Something like that, right?

I jumped through all the hoops (or most of them, at least) and did a decent job avoiding red Xs. I graduated from a good high school and a good college. I got a law degree, hoop jumping all the way.

The result of all that jumping was that, by the time I was in law school, I'd become a Creative Couch Potato. The Creative Couch Potato is a person whose creative muscles have atrophied.

Later on we'll detail the characteristics of the Creative Couch Potato, but for now let's say our education system is designed to produce Couch Potatoes capable of showing up to the factory on time and ready to follow instructions.

To be fair, the education system has had a lot of success, by certain measures. And it did contribute to the development of the most robust economy the world has ever seen. Those are very real accomplishments that arguably would not have been possible without designing the system to optimize for uniformity and compliance.

The insurmountable problem now is that we have a nineteenth-century model of education preparing twenty-first-century kids. The world and economy our education system was designed for no longer exists. The skills and traits that the existing education system optimizes for are no longer the skills and traits our children need to focus on.

WHY MORE CREATIVITY?

Even if you're on board with the case, you might still be unclear as to how creativity solves any of the problems laid out so far.

Creativity isn't so much a solution to the problems as it is an indispensable tool we need to use to solve those problems. Creativity can be our process for turning ideas into impact, our way of making beautiful little dents in the world.

Developing creativity can make a person more:

- **Resourceful:** The creative process requires making progress using what's at hand. Spending time making detailed plans of what you'd do if you won $100 million in the lottery isn't a particularly useful exercise, in that 1) you don't have $100 million, and 2) you're never going to have $100 million. Chris Guillebeau's approach of figuring out what you'd do with $100 to start making good things happen—that's being resourceful.
- **Resilient:** Because creativity is inherently about making new things, we're constantly breaking new territory. Which means that we're going to encounter a lot of dead ends. Thomas Edison had that line about how he didn't fail ten thousand times, he just learned ten thousand ways not to make a light bulb. Resilience is the ability to get back up after you get knocked down. Ten thousand times, if necessary.
- **Capable:** The creative person does work. Along the way, they develop skills. Some creatives focus on mastering

a single skill. Others focus on not focusing on a single skill, instead developing enough competence to use a range of skills. Either way, the person using their creativity can do more things better over time.

- **Disciplined:** That person is not going to be able to sit down consistently and work on those skills without developing discipline. Discipline gets a bad rap, but it's a beautiful thing. Discipline gives us command over our time, our attention, and our energy.
- **Curious:** Creativity requires paying attention to the world, noticing things that interest us, seeing where certain rabbit holes go. I believe that bored people are boring people and that interesting people are interested people (I took that from Liz Gilbert, I think). Curiosity is how we pursue what interests us.
- **Employable:** In an increasingly automated world, there will be fewer jobs available to people who simply want to show up and be told what to do all day. The economy will need people who can connect dots and solve problems, many occurring in abstract digital spaces. This is not the work the Industrial Age and its education system prepared us for, but here we are.
- **Healthy:** I believe the line about how we're either growing or dying. At its heart, my belief in the power of creativity is about always being oriented toward our growth. Keep moving. Keep learning new things. Keep exploring. Keep finding ways to open ourselves to the world. If we can do these things, the world will continue opening to us.

THE WHIPMAKER'S APPRENTICE

In 2016, I wrote the first draft of a book. The manuscript's title was *The Whipmaker's Apprentice*, and though I considered including the entire fable at the heart of that book here, I'll save you the three pages. The book was about how we have three basic ways of responding to periods of change: sticking our heads in the sand, freaking out, or learning to ride the wave of change. The whipmaker's apprentice was a young man who started working in a Michigan factory that made leather goods used primarily for carriages at the beginning of the twentieth century. The fictional company was large and immensely profitable. Then automobile manufacturers started moving into the neighborhood. The owner of the leather goods company resisted the automobiles. He found them loud, dangerous, and unsuitable to urban life.

The apprentice saw the four-wheeled contraptions differently. He saw the future. The apprentice began fiddling with designs for leather goods for autos: seat covers, steering-wheel covers, gear-shift covers, and so on. The apprentice developed his skill, and he very quickly had a market for his auto goods. He went to the owner of the leather goods company and was fired on the spot for insubordination. The owner had made his opinions of automobiles clear, and he wanted nothing to do with them.

The apprentice had intended to spend his entire working life at that company. He was crushed.

For a few days.

Then he got to work. And when the leather goods company declared bankruptcy a decade later for failing to adapt to the changing market conditions, the apprentice's automobile leather accessories business had taken off. He was a wealthy young man with a bright future because he'd had enough creativity to lean into the opportunity and the audacity to capitalize on it.

I believe that you and me and everyone we know currently sits in a position sort of like those people watching cars take over the roadways in the early 1900s.

THEN CAME THE INTERNET

The case I'm making in this book rests on a simple premise–the Industrial Age is over. The Internet has upended almost everything about how our society has operated for the last 220 years very, *very* suddenly.

How we shop.

How we work.

How we entertain ourselves.

How we communicate.

How we socialize.

How we date.

How we create.

How we learn.

How we earn.

Too many of us are watching the change happen, and the hard truth is that standing on the sidelines as the economic ground beneath our feet shifts is a terrible risk.

I heard something about the nature of employment some years back that's stuck with me. At its height in 1979, General Motors was reportedly the largest private employer in the United States, with more than 618,000 Americans. (https://www.cnbc.com/id/30962998). In 2019, Apple–one of the most successful companies on the planet–reportedly employed 90,000 people in the U.S (https://www.apple.com/newsroom/2019/08/apples-us-job-footprint-grows-to-two-point-four-million/).

It's a wild change. Now, I got that 90,000 number from the Apple website in an article claiming that Apple has an actual jobs footprint of 2.4 million in the U.S., once you account for people making their livings through the Apple ecosystem. That's an example of how the social contract of the Connection Economy will be different from that of the Industrial Age. Those wanting to show up, take orders, and collect paychecks are going to have an increasingly difficult time finding and keeping employment sufficient to provide a satisfactory quality of life and prospects for the future. I'm turning 40 this year and don't know anybody my age who's looking forward to a pension. Hell, social security seems far from a safe bet. And while it was common for our grandparents to stay at the same company for decades, very few millennials will have any frame of reference for that kind of stability.

I'm neither qualified nor inclined to make a detailed argument as to the demise of the Industrial Age. We just need to recognize–

That economy is gone.

THE CONNECTION ECONOMY

The Industrial Age has been supplanted by what entrepreneur and author Seth Godin has coined the Connection Economy.

Whereas the Industrial Economy was centralized, the Connection Economy is more decentralized. If you wanted to succeed in the Industrial Age, you had to go to the center, pass the gatekeeper. In the Connection Age, success can be determined by how many dots (and people) you connect. We gain power and influence by weaving webs of connection, taking advantage of network effects.

What we watch illustrates the point well. In the 1960s, if you had a TV, you basically had three channels–NBC, CBS, ABC. Everybody was watching the same stuff, and the makers of stuff catered what they were making to "average" people. The entertainment of the Industrial Age was the definition of mainstream.

With the rise of streaming, is there even a mainstream anymore?

Sure, we get way too many superhero movies, but we can also find whatever we want to watch, no matter how esoteric our tastes or interests.

That game has changed. So has the economy.

OFFSCRIPTING

In May 2013, I gave notice at the law firm in downtown St. Louis where I was an associate. I intended to spend a year traveling around Southeast Asia. I sold my car, got rid of my apartment, prepared to live out of a single backpack.

Up until that point, I had walked the well-trodden, comfortable path to success. I colored inside the lines and checked the right boxes. I got decent grades and interviewed well. The path works for a lot of people. It didn't work for me. I can't say that I wanted a better path, but I did want a different path.

By 2015, my one year of a sabbatical had stretched to more than two years, courtesy of attorney contract work. My sister Christie had taken a similar path, and we started a blog called Offscripting. The basic premise—If the conventional script for success has you feeling unfulfilled or stuck, it might be time to veer from it and start writing your own story.

For the two years we actively ran that blog, we preached about the value of offscripting as a method of self-discovery. We didn't specifically think about what we were doing in creative terms, but we were describing a way of approaching our futures as blank canvases.

Where to travel.

What to work on.

Which career path to take.

Everything was open for consideration.

We were collecting and connecting dots.

At the time, we limited our proclamation to talking about what worked for us as individuals. We were careful to include disclaimers about how we had no problems with the conventional path.

Six years later, I do have more of a problem with the conventional path—It's disappearing.

I BELIEVE

The world needs more people strengthening their creative muscles.

School attempted to squash our creativity because the industrial society needed obedient workers more than it needed creative individuals.

The world has changed and the Industrial Era is over, but too many people and systems, including the education system, have been slow to get the message.

In the Industrial Age, raising your head above the herd was a good way to lose your head.

In the Connection Economy, it's the only way to get ahead.

In a world of increasing automation, the robots will do more and more. We need to be learning how to help one another in ways the robots won't be so capable of doing better and quicker and cheaper.

The economy of tomorrow is here today, and it's one that rewards creativity.

In the Connection Economy, the spoils will go to the most creative, the risk-takers, the trailblazers, those willing to dare greatly, adapt on the fly, experiment, and create.

The future belongs to the Creative Contenders, the creative in the arena.

So does the present.

If you're not a Contender today, that's all right. But I'd recommend that you start taking action immediately to work toward being a Contender tomorrow.

PART II

Becoming a Creative Contender

WHAT'S A CREATIVE COUCH POTATO?

Let's consider some of the Creative Couch Potato's characteristics:

They love consuming but don't do much creating.

They want to get the right answer as quickly as possible—learning is secondary.

They want to avoid wasting time or, god forbid, arriving at wrong answers on the path to a right answer.

They want a linear path to success. After jumping through hoops all the way through school, they'd like to continue on the same trajectory until retirement.

They choose a template kind of life, one with seemingly low risk and a predictable future.

It's worth noting that not all people whose lives look like that above qualify as Creative Couch Potatoes. As Mason Currey in *Daily Rituals* recalled de Balzac saying, let your life's routines be predictable and mundane so that your creativity can be wild.

The determining factor in whether you're a Creative Couch Potato is whether you feel like you're keeping a substantial part of yourself on the shelf. The Creative Couch Potato knows on some level that they've chosen an easier, softer path, not out of desire but out of fear. They choose the template life, the well-trodden conventional path to success, because to attempt anything different carries substantially more risk of failure. At the very least, such a choice requires a willingness to fail, which is something the Creative Couch Potato cannot fathom or abide. By the time I finished law school in 2009, I certainly couldn't abide failure.

THE CREATIVE CONTENDER

The Creative Contender may not have achieved notoriety, fame, or fortune yet, but she is creatively fit. She knows what she's about and can be counted on to show up and do her Work. She is building a Body of Work that can be engaged with and, for better or worse, judged.

Ever heard about how you can accurately predict someone's wealth by averaging the wealths of that person's five closest friends?

I don't know if it's true, but it makes sense.

The same goes for Creative Contenders.

You show me your five closest friends, and I'll be able to tell you whether you're a Creative Contender without ever having met you.

Because I know what a Contender looks like. And Contenders tend to run with their own.

Let's consider the characteristics of the Contender.

THE CONTENDER
AND RESILIENCE

The Contender has been knocked down in the creative arena and knows that the cliche is true: what matters isn't how many times you get knocked down but how many times you get back up.

The Contender has failed, tasted rejection, been outright ignored. You know all those feelings.

The Contender knows defeat and even welcomes it (in our grander moments). Every defeat is a lesson and a step toward the top of the mountain.

THE CONTENDER
AND PATIENCE

The Contender understands that overnight successes don't happen overnight. I don't know who said it first, but "The overnight success was ten years in the making" is spot on. The Contender is playing the long game and embraces that, six years in, you're right where you need to be. Success isn't around the next corner, but you're at least moving in its direction. While it's possible you end up in a maze and never actually reach Success, you know that you're not yet close enough to the destination to reach a conclusion about the value of your Work.

To prematurely demand market validation would be like a traveler on a road trip from Los Angeles to New York City declaring that NYC isn't nearly as impressive as expected—from Pittsburgh.

THE CONTENDER
AND CONSISTENCY

The Contender shows up, rain or shine. Day after day. Week after week. We aren't perfect. Not every wrestling match with Resistance is a win. A consistently solid baseball player might have a .300 batting average year after year over a number of seasons. That's an excellent track record.

It also means he failed to get a hit in 7 out of every 10 at bats. To be a Contender, we need to win the daily wrestling match more than 30 percent of the time (I think), but who am I to say where that line is?

The Contender takes the Work seriously. You're going to show up to do your Work because you know that it's worth doing and that it won't get done if you don't do it. Like The Pro described by Pressfield in *The War of Art*, you have a blue-collar mentality about your Work. It might be fine art or high design, but your mindset is simple, austere even.

Show up.

Do the Work.

THE CONTENDER AND INDEPENDENCE

The Contender knows that most people won't understand, and that's all right.

By the time a creative reaches Contender status, they also have some idea what they're doing in terms of the craft. The Contender has put in the time and the effort to learn technique, to study the masters who have come before. It's only by learning from the past that we can create something valuable and new for the future. Newton wrote, "If I have seen further, it is by standing on the shoulders of giants. The Contender knows what Newton's talking about. Our Work comes through us, but it is not from us.

The Contender also knows that the best Work tends to come not from an exultation of the ego but from a letting go of ego that allows us to connect with the world beyond ourselves. We are at our best when we're channeling the energy of the universe and all the giants who have come before.

In Ken Burns' documentary *Jazz*, there's a moment where an interviewer asks Duke Ellington where he gets his ideas.

"The ideas? Oh man, I got a million dreams. That's all I do is dream. All the time."

"I heard you play piano."

"No, this is not piano. This is dreaming."

To be able to dream in public, the Contender knows that the homework needs to get done. The medium needs attention and study. The craft needs development.

THE CONTENDER
AND HUMILITY

Ideally, every Creative Contender has humility, which I define as having a right-sized attitude about yourself. A humble person doesn't think too highly or too lowly of themselves. In essence, it's about recognizing that we're all human, just out here trying to do the best we can.

Simultaneously, the Contender knows that none of us know what we're doing. We can't know ahead of time which projects will work and which won't. Even the greatest of creatives—from Beethoven to Hemingway—were terrible at predicting which works would succeed. This is not a coincidence, and it is not an indictment either of the creative making the Work or the public judging it. This is a natural feature of the creative process. The Contender knows to focus on the process that produces the Work to be shipped.

THE CONTENDER
AND PROGRESS

And finally, the Contender has a shot at making it. You might not have reached the mountaintop yet, but you have put in the time and effort to get some skills. You understand yourself and your Resistance well enough to win that daily battle consistently. The Contender has creatives to look up to, but there might also be some people looking up to you. The Contender isn't guaranteed to win, to succeed.

But the Contender is in the arena. The Contender is going to shoot their shots and take their chances. Then let the chips fall as they may.

The postscript is that the Contender has an inkling of a truth passed down from previous contenders, that the mountaintop does not mark the end of the journey. It's just a resting point. The next peak looms in the distance, waiting. The Contender can savor the pleasure in this moment—but only for a moment. Because the joy of the Contender is not in the arriving but in the doing, the making, the creating.

Are you a Creative Contender?

No?

Not yet?

Then we've got some work to do.

THE CONTENDER
AND CURIOSITY

Do you know what curiosity means? It means wanting to know more about the world. Some people get curious about one thing and spend a lifetime going deeper and deeper into that thing. These are called specialists or experts. Some people get curious about a lot of different things at the same time and learn some stuff about all of them along the way. These people are generalists. I'm one of those.

Some Creative Contenders are specialists. Some are generalists.

All Contenders are curious.

THE CONTENDER
AND COURAGE

This might not be the best word for what we're aiming at here, but until we find a better one, courage will just have to do. As Brené Brown has described it, courage is feeling fear and doing the thing anyway. Creative Contenders know that doing Work can be intimidating, even frightening.

Doing the Work can be scary, in that we might end up exploring parts of ourselves or the world that get dark. And shipping Work is often scary. In certain mediums, repetition helps strengthen the shipping muscle, and the fear diminishes with practice. Posting writing on LinkedIn has been like that for me. Initially, pressing that Publish button evoked a little bit of anxiety in me (What if they don't like it? What if they don't even read it? What if they fire me?). Now, it's just what I do.

But Steven Pressfield includes an anecdote about Henry Fonda, one of the greatest American actors, in *The War of Art*. Even at the age of seventy-five, Fonda would vomit in his dressing room before going out on stage for a play. He had been acting for more than half a century and won every award there was to win, and he still felt it.

THE CONTENDER
AND ACCEPTANCE

The Contender knows that nothing is promised in this game of making change. You make what you do without any promises that you will see the desired results.

The Contender understands what Krishna told Arjuna on the battlefield in the Bhagavad Gita: you are entitled to the labor but not the fruits of the labor.

Creative work requires that we focus on the inputs, the only things we can control. The Contender focuses on controllable inputs. You can't control whether a tire on the car goes flat or the ten query letters for your manuscript go unanswered. You do, however, have some control over whether you put in the time today. So you do that. And tomorrow? You do it again, knowing that with each passing day, putting in the Work, you become a fuller version of your creative self, and you get better at your craft.

To spend our time or energy worrying about outputs and outcomes will lead to nothing but pain and potentially paralysis.

THE PROGRESSION

So we've established that creativity is essentially a process for making things happen in the real world. And it's important because—at the risk of sounding alarmist—our society's social contract promising jobs with pensions and a career's worth of workdays has evaporated.

What do you do about it?

My suggestion is that you (and I) should become Creative Contenders.

We were raised to be Creative Couch Potatoes, to consume and watch and accept. It has led us to a generation (or two) of people who are woefully unprepared and ill-equipped for a rapidly changing, volatile environment. Which is precisely what we're living in right now.

Frankly, I believe Gen Zers are figuring this out on the fly. Or maybe it's due to the combination of social media, which allows everyone to be thinking creatively all day long, and no illusions that we millennials were seduced with as to the benefits of the conventional path to success. As I write these sentences, I'm seeing a rabbit hole comparing generations begging me to jump in; I'm not going to do it. There's no way I'm qualified to wax philosophic on those questions at any length, and it doesn't matter.

Regardless of when you were born or how many TikToks you've made, the fact remains that you need to be getting in shape creatively, putting in the work to go from Couch Potato to Contender.

I've laid out my own personal experience with this shift, and the rest of this book is going to lay out, in detail uncharacteristic for my ADHD brain, how a person so inclined could strengthen their creative muscles.

The way I see it, getting in shape creatively looks pretty much the same as doing it physically. I've run some longer distances in my life, and training for a thirty-mile run requires that I focus on developing three things:

1) Mindset: Approach my days as a runner. Runners run. Runners eat right. Runners rely on routine and discipline.

2) Exercise: Hard to succeed on race day without having put in the miles, week by week, over an extended period of time. I do longer, slower runs to build up stamina and shorter, fast runs to build lung capacity. I do bodyweight and core work to strengthen and solidify my middle.

3) Diet: I once read something that said going crazy on one meal can eliminate the benefits of five days of workouts. I have no idea whether that's true and, if it is, I'm totally screwed. But it's undeniable that what I put into my body has an impact on my ability to ask my body to perform at a certain level in a particular way.

If I cut corners in any of those three areas, my training will suffer, which will then lead to my suffering (more) on race day.

INTERNAL VS. EXTERNAL

Becoming a Contender requires paying attention both to what's going on inside as well as what's going on outside your mind and body.

The internal component is largely about learning to show up for your daily wrestling match with Resistance ready to give it a run for its money. We're going to talk about Resistance at some length, but essential to getting your mind right as a creative is to understand that:

1. There is a daily battle against Resistance;
2. Many of us spend much of our lives not even fighting it; and
3. Showing up is roughly 91 percent of the battle.

In *The War of Art*, Pressfield wrote about a secret that wannabe writers don't know. The secret is that "it's not the writing part that's hard. It's the sitting down to write. And what keeps us from sitting down is Resistance."

It's that moment of sitting down that provides the inflection point between the internal work and the external work of getting creatively fit. The lifting required to simply put your butt in the seat day after day is an internal challenge, a mental and spiritual one.

Wrapped up in those three things I listed above are a couple questions that every creative needs to answer to have a chance at sustaining their work over time.

What does Resistance look like for you?

What are you afraid of?

I believe that the internal struggle is pretty much that simple. Know what Resistance looks like for you, and know what scares you.

It might not sound like much, but it'll keep you busy for the rest of your days.

Once you know what Resistance looks like, you can start to strategize how to avoid those specific pitfalls. Once you acknowledge all the things you're afraid of—both creatively and beyond—you can give those fears their due for trying to keep you safe while then also going on and doing your Work. Getting all that stuff out into the open—at least in the open between your ears, where you're aware of it—can diminish its power.

The external component of getting in shape consists of not just what you might call the exercises or regimen but also the routines and settings of your creative life. The where, when, what, and how of getting your Work done. By establishing routines and order in your creative life, you increase the likelihood that you will succeed in putting your butt in the seat on a given day. Resistance has fewer places to hide.

When you know what the battle today looks like and clearly understand your strategy for winning today, you're on your way to being a Creative Contender.

WHAT IS RESISTANCE?

I've debated how much detail to provide on this question because my short answer is:

Go read *The War of Art* by Steven Pressfield, a book I've already referred to several times here.

The War of Art changed my creative life in ways that I've yet to fully understand, and I've gifted it to people more than any other book. Let's spend a bit of time outlining it here.

As Pressfield defines it, Resistance is a natural force that pushes back against us whenever we try to do anything to improve ourselves or the world. Resistance is the little devil on our shoulder. Resistance is Couch Potato Tony, whispering that I can run those ten miles or write those ten pages tomorrow and today I should eat a bag of cookies and try to watch an entire season of *Seinfeld*.

Resistance is tricky, cunning, and extremely adaptive. Resistance can show up at any time, and it can shapeshift depending on circumstances. Sometimes Resistance looks like procrastination, sometimes drama, sometimes distraction.

There's some debate as to whether Resistance is nefarious or even evil in some way. Pressfield declares Resistance evil because, as he puts it, Resistance tries to keep us from realizing our full potential on our way back to God. Framed that way, Resistance doesn't just sound like the little devil on the shoulder— Resistance *is* the devil.

I find that framing a little intense and, ultimately, unhelpful. If I think about my personal battle against Resistance in terms of a cosmic battle of good versus evil, my ego kicks into high gear (I have problems stemming from a historically inflated sense of self), and I start thinking like a hero. This immediately leads to a problem—I'm not a hero, and my work doesn't feel in the least bit heroic, especially in the moment. At which point I realize that there's no way I'm going to be able to contend with the devil, much less win, so why try?

That's a win for Resistance.

For me, winning my battle against Resistance consistently depends largely on my framing Resistance not as nefarious but as natural. Resistance is like gravity. Sure, gravity keeps me from flying, and flying would be cool, but gravity doesn't root for my failure in flying, nor does it have any intention to keep me from flying. Gravity is unaware of my existence and is just doing what gravity does.

Same with Resistance.

Resistance isn't out to get me. It's not the devil.

It's just the natural force pushing back against me.

With intention and effort and discipline, though, we can jujitsu Resistance from being an adversary or enemy into the primary mechanism by which we make progress.

WHAT'S RESISTANCE LOOK LIKE

The War of Art rocked my world because, when I read Pressfield's description of Resistance in its many forms, I knew what he was talking about instantly and intimately. Suddenly, twenty years of nonsense snapped into place in a new way of understanding the world.

Until that point, I had concerns that I was a degenerate of sorts, that my struggles to make progress creatively stemmed not from circumstance or some external force but from some undeniable, uncorrectable deficiency within. And that's still possible, of course.

But Resistance gave me language to process what I'd previously chalked up to character defects. Once that happened, it got a lot easier to identify what Resistance looked like—and what to do about it.

Resistance can look like a lot of things. Your Resistance might not look much like my Resistance. My Resistance today might not look like my Resistance yesterday. But here are some of the ways Resistance presents for me:

- Procrastination: Why do today what can be put off until tomorrow?
- Distraction: Shiny objects in the moment (iPhone, anyone?) and shiny new projects that look far more attractive than the current one.
- Drama: There is very little in the world as effective to keep me doing my work than some exciting interpersonal conflict.

- Perfectionism: Good enough is *not* good enough. This thing must not just be a good thing but the *best* of things. And no less than the best will do.
- Self-Doubt: What's the point of even finishing something if nobody is going to see it and anybody who does see it will most certainly hate it?
- Snacking: Mmmmmmmmmm.

Those would be my greatest hits. I know them now. I know what they are. Which gives me more power to know what to do about them.

A DIAGNOSIS

Stop me if you've heard this one.

A guy goes to the doctor.

"Doc, you've gotta help me. I've got ten different things going on, and I'm so sick I can't get anything done. It's killin' me!"

"What are your symptoms?" the doctor asks.

"More like, what aren't my symptoms!

I've got rashes.

I'm tired all the time.

I've got this sore on my lip that won't go away.

I've got a sore throat, and my lymph nodes are swollen something fierce.

I've been dropping weight for no reason.

Little bumps have popped up on my body.

And I've got a weird, you know . . . down there."

The doctor checks the guy out, runs some tests, and comes back.

"Well, I've got some good news and some bad news."

"Gimme the good news."

"The good news is you don't have ten things wrong with you."

"Oh? Then what's the bad news?"

"You do have syphilis."

MY OWN BOUT OF RESISTANCE

I had an acute case of Resistance through much of my twenties.

My Symptoms
- I'm too busy with work to write.
- I'm just not feeling inspired.
- I'm too tired.
- I'll work on the story tomorrow.
- It would be good to write, but I should probably get *drunk* first.
- I need more excitement to spark inspiration—I should go start a fight with my girlfriend.
- Ugh, my girlfriend is so mad at me because I picked a fight with her. I can't write.
- I need the perfect font and will now spend fifteen minutes manually changing the font on this one sentence fifty times.
- This chair is too hard/soft/high/low/chairy. Let's go chair shopping.

I wanted to be a writer through college, majored in English Composition, wrote columns for the weekly newspaper and short stories in creative writing classes. By the time I was graduating from undergrad, however, Resistance was already having its way with me. I wanted to be a writer, yet somehow my capstone project for my bachelor's ended up being a thirty-six36-page paper about political strategist Karl Rove. Pretty good paper, but a peculiar choice for a young man with literary aspirations.

I did not run across the term Resistance until well into my thirties (more on that momentarily), but I now can clearly see the symptoms my twenty-four24-year-old self had—, all the things that kept him from writing.

All that to say, Resistance would find any reason it could to keep me from writing. Through my twenties, I did indeed, as the bard Jay-Z said, have 99 problems.

In reality, I had one problem.

Resistance.

. . . And just to be clear, I do not have—and have never have had—syphilis.

I can't state that strongly enough.

YOUR RESISTANCE

Once I learned what Resistance could look like, I suddenly started seeing it everywhere, just like how you'll start seeing red Subarus everywhere the minute you start thinking about buying a red Subaru. That included looking back into my past. So many instances that had been attributed to bad luck or bad relationships or bad timing or not enough inspiration now all snapped into place—I'd lost the battle against Resistance.

Do you know what Resistance looks like for you?

If I asked you to list out all the ways Resistance shows up in your life, pushing against you when you're trying to do something worthwhile, how long a list would you have?

It's a worthwhile exercise.

LISTING RESISTANCE

- Get a piece of paper and a writing utensil.
- Set a timer for eight minutes.
- Write down as many forms of Resistance as you can. Don't worry about getting words precisely right. The point is to explicitly notice any habit, activity, character trait, or behavior that has a tendency to get in the way of you doing your creative Work.
- After eight minutes, put it aside.
- Add to the list during the next three days as new items for the list come to mind.

That simple exercise can do a couple things for you.

First, it can help you break negative habits. The more aware I become that I have a tendency to procrastinate, the more likely I become to take action to remedy it.

Second, you can start to see the world through a lens of identifying Resistance. It will become easier to spot. That's not good for Resistance because the more you notice it, the more time and energy you'll be putting into winning that wrestling match. Resistance is pretty good at what it does. It's resourceful, cunning, amorally flexible, and indefatigable.

But it's not undefeatable. Every time you put butt in the seat and Do. The. Work., you beat Resistance for that day. And winning on a given day, when done with intention and understanding, can indeed mean it's more likely that you'll win again tomorrow.

That's really our goal with getting creatively fit, isn't it? We want to be able to show up day after day after day and make good stuff happen.

THE KEY TO BEATING RESISTANCE

I've never been a fan of lifting weights.

Because I've never been a fan of lifting weights, I've lifted very few weights in my life. I was an athlete in high school but spent as little time as possible in weight rooms. And because I never liked it and have been so effective in not lifting weights, I've never been very strong in my upper body.

I wanted to be strong. Having a strong upper body would have provided benefits valuable to me.

But because I didn't like the discomfort of being weak and the negative feelings associated with that—comparison to stronger people, fear of judgment, self-doubt about my ability to ever get stronger—I avoided doing the thing that could have helped me overcome all those negative feelings and the discomfort.

I missed the plot.

The way to overcome those challenges was not to avoid them. I should have leaned into that challenge, which was, in that case, essentially about gravity *and* Resistance. Resistance had its way with me so that I wouldn't do the work required to learn how to impose my will on gravity a little more by lifting bits of metal over my head.

Making progress creatively isn't all that different.

Understand the nature of the challenge in front of you.

Improving creatively and making more Work isn't done by going around Resistance or avoiding it or eliminating it.

We must face Resistance. We must move through

Resistance.

And we must do that every day. Which is maybe the main reason I choose to view Resistance not as an evil enemy but as a friendly sibling I've always known and will always know. We're not locked in a vicious struggle to the death. No, we just have daily wrestling matches. I want to win those matches. I want to win every single one. I want to go undefeated, and I want to do it with style and panache.

But I always know that tomorrow will be another chance to try my luck and test my skill. To view Resistance as an enemy is to turn your life into a never-ending struggle against a malevolent force you face off with on the daily.

That sounds exhausting. And depressing.

Enemies are to be destroyed.

Siblings are to be lived with (and cherished, if you've got sisters like mine!)

And deep down, if I'm being honest, I don't *always* want to win. Every once in a while I won't say I throw a match, but I might not try quite as hard. I might sort of take the day off, let Resistance have its way. Not because I want to stroke Resistance's ego or make it feel better about itself, but because my own ego needs a little checking from time to time. If I get too dominant, I might start to believe my own press, and that's not good for anybody. Humility in the struggle, staying mindful of the reality that victory is not —and should not be—guaranteed, helps keep me grounded and primed for today's match.

WHAT ARE YOU AFRAID OF

You might not be like me, but I have a good deal of fear when it comes to my creative life. It's possibly too much fear, or more fear than is reasonable, given that my primary medium of creative expression has been writing, and there's very little that is actually dangerous about writing or typing words on a sheet of real or digital paper.

But that's not really true, is it?

Because writing—and I'd argue, any genuine creative expression—involves exposing yourself to the world. When we open ourselves up, we're vulnerable. Critics and bullies can take aim and fire not just at us but at the parts of us that feel more essential in some way, more needing of protection.

As a creative, I'm afraid of a lot.

Rejection.

Being exposed as a fraud.

Failure.

Wasting my time.

It not working.

And, oddly enough, success.

Because what might happen if I were to stop playing small?

The stakes go way up in a hurry. That prospect gets my heart beating a little faster just typing these words.

THE CHALLENGE OF ACTUALLY DOING WORK

I said somewhere up there that learning to win the internal battle has a disproportionate impact on a person's ability to win the daily battle against Resistance and do their Work. That being said, *only* improving on the internal front will not get you far, right? At some point, once we've put our butt in the seat, we have to actually Do. The. Work. This is the diet and exercise portion of our program—the actions we take that lead to Work getting done.

It's fairly simple stuff but not necessarily easy. Because, for almost all of us, the creative Work we're talking about needs to be worked into a schedule that doesn't have too many obvious holes —blocks of time conducive to getting Work done. For instance, I'm typing these words with the laptop on my lap in the front seat of our Subaru Forester. It is 5:49 a.m., and my toddler daughter is asleep in the back seat. She's at an incredibly cute age, and also an age where her sleep schedule is whack. She will go to sleep at a reasonable time, 7:30 p.m. or so, and then wake up crying at 4:30 or 5 a.m. She's not ready to be up yet, but if we leave her in the crib, she will not go back to sleep. She will just proceed from crying to wailing.

So during the last ten days writing this manuscript, I have loaded her into the car and driven a little bit until she falls back asleep. I then park and bang out a thousand words.

Almost all of this book's first draft will have been written in this manner.

Far cry from Hemingway in the attic hunched over his desk for eight hours a day, isn't it?

And that's my point. I ain't Hemingway. And my hunch is that you ain't Hemingway either.

You're somebody with a job. Maybe it's a 9 to 5. Maybe you're a hustler, a freelancer or a solopreneur, which means you have no boss—you have more like twelve bosses. So, sure, you have flexibility over when you work, but you're probably working a lot.

You have a family. A spouse or partner. Kids. Various animals that rely on you. Then there are the other commitments involved in being a person who is alive in a society. Going out with friends. Getting to the gym. Doing the mundane nonsense demanded of us by the DMV or the tax man or the doctor. Sleeping once in a while.

On top of all of that, almost every single person reading this carries in their pocket a supercomputer, an incredibly powerful device designed to consume as much of your time and attention as possible. The Netflix documentary *The Social Dilemma* made an obvious but essential point: It's not a fair fight. We're basically advanced apes wearing pants, and these are devices more powerful than anything Bill Clinton had at his disposal as the de facto most powerful person on Earth as recently as the 1990s.

Which is to say, when we're not occupied doing all the things involved in living, our attention tends to get sucked toward that device, one minute at a time.

Have I painted a sufficiently bleak picture when it comes to figuring out how to find time to get creatively fit?

Good.

Understanding the challenge allows us to determine whether it's important enough to try. If something is worth doing —or at least worth attempting—then we need to be willing to fight for the time, the space, and the energy to put toward the doing.

Which brings me back to Hemingway. I reflexively refer to him because he was the ideal of the Great American Writer that got lodged in my impressionable brain back in high school. To be honest with you, I don't even know how often he managed to spend six hours alone in an attic room. Maybe that was only a short time of his life. But I read a book about him somewhere along the way, and that image stuck. What also stuck is the idea that *that's* how a writer writes. Alone. For extended periods of time.

That's not how it works for me doing my Work these days. That's probably not how it's going to work for you. And that's all right. We can do our Work in fifteen- or thirty-minute increments. Might take us a little longer to get where we're going, but I assure you that you'll get a lot further with your Work at fifteen minutes per day than you would if you weren't doing it at all because you can't set aside four hours every day.

J. D. Salinger was another of those Great American Writers I idolized. *The Catcher in the Rye* is a book I revisit with some regularity, and I'm always impressed at how well it holds up. I was blown away at fifteen years old by the attention to detail, and I still am as I push forty.

The kicker about that book is that Salinger was working on it while—quite literally—fighting Nazis. Salinger was an intelligence officer in the US Army and spent 1944 and 1945 careening from one momentous event of that war to the next. He was at the Battle of the Bulge. He was at the liberation of the Dachau concentration camp. He was at the Nuremberg trials.

All along the way, chapters of *The Catcher in the Rye* were tucked away in his pack. He would write in his down time. My understanding is that war often involves a lot of down time, many extended periods of intense boredom punctuated by relatively brief bursts of horrific activity. Salinger would write on a table or his lap somewhere, fifteen minutes at a time if necessary.

You and I are (I hope) lucky enough to not have our own mortality hanging in the balance today, so our challenge is far more mundane. But it's not totally different. We're trying to find the gaps between the activity where we can Work. Then maybe, if we're even luckier, we might eventually get to the point where, if we so choose, we have the freedom to spend six hours in an attic hunched over a desk, banging away on the keyboard.

Until that happens, though, we're going to have to play the

hand we've been dealt. This section of the book is written as if you're someone with various demands on your time and energy. We're going to talk about finding or carving out those little bits of time that will allow you to make progress one day at a time.

ONE MORE WORD ABOUT SALINGER

Before we move on, another word about how wild it is that Salinger wrote part of *The Catcher in the Rye* in Europe during WWII. This goes without saying, but he very easily could have been killed with an unfinished manuscript in his pocket. I shudder to think of how much creative potential was lost in that war, in addition to the loss of life.

He didn't know whether he would survive the war and wrote under the veil of that uncertainty. I wonder how that reality affected him.

Did it paralyze him?

Or did it motivate him?

THE URGENCY OF CREATIVITY

I've never been to war, but I do spend what might be an unhealthy amount of time thinking about my mortality.

I am going to die.

It's the most obvious of statements, yet also at least a little uncomfortable. It seems that we understand the idea intellectually but have a difficult time contemplating a world without us in it. When I think about my pending demise, my mind quickly gets to the point:

What am I doing to make the most of my time here?

Am I putting enough of my time and energy into the relationships that really matter?

Am I taking the risks that, at the end of the day, might make the flame of my life worth the candle required to produce it?

Am I creating anything of value, something that can make even the tiniest of beautiful dents in this world and have a positive impact on somebody?

Am I even putting in the Work necessary to create something of value?

In Howard Zinn's phenomenal book, *A People's History of the United States*, there's a story about the American writers Henry David Thoreau and Ralph Waldo Emerson. Thoreau once refused to pay a tax as a protest against slavery and the Mexican-American War, a conflict he saw as unjust and imperialistic. He lived in Concord, a small Massachusetts town where just about everybody knew everybody else, and Thoreau ended up getting taken to the town jail.

Emerson, a more pragmatic man (but aren't we all more pragmatic than the man whose claim to fame involves a book about living alone for a year in a cabin on Walden Pond), did not approve of the protest, thinking it useless. He is said to have walked up to the window of Thoreau's jail cell and looked in.

"Henry, what are you doing in there?"

Thoreau, without skipping a beat, responded:

"Waldo, the question is, what are you doing out there?"

I liked the line so much that I had it tattooed across my left forearm in script that I now understand to be far larger than necessary (it was my second tattoo). The tattoo is a reminder to not get too comfortable in my privilege, to be mindful of the need to be on the right side of things, especially when it's uncomfortable for me.

But the line can extend to our creative Work and what it means to embark on a life well lived.

When that voice of the Couch Potato asks what you're doing in there, working on writing a book or starting a website, we can respond:

"What are you doing out there, Creative Couch Potato?!"

We do it not because we're guaranteed to win or succeed or have the thing work. We do it because it's in us and wants to come out, because doing the Work makes us a better version of ourselves.

We do it because we are, indeed, going to die, and we will not be stopped from doing our damnedest to contribute between now and our last day.

MINDSET

I would not be writing this book if I hadn't heard Seth Godin mention Steven Pressfield's *The War of Art* on a podcast in 2015. My hunch is there are a number of things I wouldn't have made. *The War of Art* is the book I recommend more than any other because of how its premise changed my outlook.

That premise: To make progress creatively, you must learn, first and foremost, how to win the daily battle against Resistance. If you can figure out how to do that, you will make Work. If you make Work, you have a chance at succeeding, whatever success means to you.

And as it turns out, the hardest part about getting in shape creatively is most likely becoming a beast at sitting down in the first place.

WORKOUTS

What happens once you succeed in sitting down to do your Work can look like workouts. They require concentrated amounts of energy. It helps if they're timed. Doing them consistently is critical to getting better and stronger at what you do.

I think about these workouts as falling into a couple different buckets. One bucket is general, and the other is domain specific. The general bucket is about simply getting the creative muscles moving without working on a project that has a specific end goal. Journaling is an example. It can strengthen the discipline muscle and the writing muscle, but you're not intending to have something publishable at the end.

In the other bucket are exercises directed typically at projects. How to lift in a way that produces your novel or your painting or your website.

A CREATIVE DIET

You are what you eat. Yada Yada.

We all know that a bad diet will lead to unhealthy bodies. You likely don't need me to tell you that the same goes for your mind. Your creative diet can help you get more and new and better ideas. It can help dots connect and problems resolve.

Of course, maintaining a healthy creative diet in this culture is about as challenging as staying on the straight and narrow when it comes to food. We live in a junk food culture, don't we? It's easier and cheaper to eat at McDonald's than just about anywhere else. Mentally, we're inundated with mental junk food. The rise of the smartphone has connected our brains to a potentially endless stream of neural sugar.

If we let it. So we need to not let our brains consume only junk food.

I'm not opposed to Netflix. I consider myself fairly in shape creatively but have been known to binge shows (Yellowstone, most recently).

I'm not puritanical about this stuff but understand that if I want to get the ideas and solutions I need to keep making progress creatively, I need to be filling my head with nutritional stuff intellectually—and then also having periods of time where I'm not putting anything in my head, where I'm leaving space and silence for the Muse to drop something into my brain.

CREATIVE MUSCLES

There are roughly six hundred muscles in the human body.

How many creative muscles are there in a human person?

Hell if I know. We're going to focus on some of the muscles I can readily identify and know will help you get to contender status.

The seven muscles we'll be considering are the big ones associated with your creative process:

- Generating ideas
- Selecting ideas
- Starting projects
- Beginning days
- Unquitting
- Finishing
- Polishing
- Shipping

Let's consider them one by one. We're not going to get too deep on these. I'll give you a sense of how I think about them and a tip for focusing on them. We'll get into more detail about how to strengthen them later on when we get into the creative workouts.

GENERATING IDEAS

If you want to get good ideas, you need to make a lot of ideas. That's a line from Seth Godin that has stuck with me for the better part of a decade, after spending my formative years believing the opposite, that my goal should be to come up with *one* brilliant, undeniable idea, and then executing on that.

I have such an idea for a novel. It's tentatively titled T*he All-American*. You've never read it because no more than ten pages have ever been written. I got precious with the idea of that book to a degree that prevented me from writing it. It was pretty much my only idea for a book between the ages of twenty-two and thirty-one.

Since then, I've gotten a bunch of book ideas. I've got drafts of two others. The one you're reading is my third drafted book and first published. I've also had a ridiculous amount of ideas for websites, businesses, songs, events, communities. It is by getting a bunch of ideas (and starting down a lot of rabbit holes) that I get a better sense of what I can make that might actually be good.

SELECTING IDEAS

The flip side to this strategy of producing good ideas is that you're going to end up with a mountain of bad ideas—ideas that simply will not work. As we get more creative, it seems that the problem becomes less about getting ideas and more about exercising prudence in determining which ideas we pursue.

A weird thing about getting ideas is how often I'm under the impression that the idea I just had is truly brilliant. My impulse is to get excited about a new idea, as if the Muse has indeed kissed me. Way too many of my ideas feel like genuine light-bulb moments in the moment.

It's only after sleeping on an idea (maybe for a while) and bouncing it off somebody else (maybe a few somebody elses) that I might have a more accurate perspective on an idea's merit.

I learned this lesson about pumping the brakes on my own ideas the hard way, and it still stings enough, six years later, that I cringe at including it here. I had an idea for what was essentially a T-shirt company. I cared deeply about the endeavor and dove in with aplomb. I built out a landing page, hired a designer for a logo, and got quotes on making T-shirts—a lot of T-shirts. My beautiful and brilliant wife suggested that I order a small batch of T-shirts, a proof-of-concept run.

I didn't need proof of concept. I knew the world needed not just T-shirts but *these* T-shirts.

Five hundred.

I ordered five hundred T-shirts.

And sold twenty-three of them. Total. The rest sat in boxes and trash bags in basements and storage units for years. The last of them landed in a Goodwill donation bin in 2021. That felt good, in the same way that it feels good when you stop banging your head against the wall.

STARTING PROJECTS

When it comes to creative projects, some people find starting to be terribly challenging. Others dread finishing. I fall squarely into the latter category and, frankly, have a hard time understanding the fear of starting. To me, there's little in life as energizing as starting a new creative project: breaking the seal on chapter one of a new book, buying a new website domain, booking the plane ticket for that next trip. But starting can be intimidating, can't it?

If Resistance has gotten its way for any length of time, then you might be in a spot where you don't even show up for the wrestling match. Resistance can kick back and hang out, knowing you won't be trying to get any Work done. And if you somehow got a wild idea, your creative muscles aren't strong enough to get you past the starting line.

Before we even take a step, we find reasons not to proceed. We're not ready. We don't have the proper equipment or materials. We don't yet know how the story ends. We have so much going on at work this week.

Starting is simultaneously easy and, at times, herculean in its demands on us.

What's the first step on that project?

Take that one step. Then you're in a different place and can figure out what happens next. You're the hero on the Hero's Journey, stepping from the familiar into the Dark Wood.

BEGINNING DAYS

I become increasingly less likely to write with every passing minute after I wake up. If I get to 11 a.m. and still haven't written, I'm not at all confident that it'll happen, which gives Resistance more leverage to work with. But when I start my day with my writing session, Resistance hasn't really had a chance to get itself sorted. It's almost like I can catch Resistance off guard. It's got its strengths, but Resistance can be beaten.

Beating Resistance once is all well and good, but getting any project to the finish line requires stringing together one day after another where progress gets made. You're in the Dark Wood, and the only acceptable way out is through, one step at a time. For me, writing this book is not so much one project as it is twenty-five different writing sessions.

The clearer I can get as to my writing schedule, the more likely I am to actually put Butt in Seat and do the writing. I'm not saying you need to do your creative Work at 5 a.m., but it helps to understand where your Work happens and when.

UNQUITTING

Whether you become a Contender isn't about how many times you get knocked down. It's about how many times you get back up. Regardless of how confident we are as creatives or how many projects we've shipped, we think about quitting a lot. There's nothing wrong with quitting. In Seth Godin's *The Dip*, he suggests that quitting is a good thing. The problem is that we quit the wrong things at the wrong times.

Quitting skateboarding or ballet or the Scouts is one thing. We typically just grow out of those.

Quitting your novel, your business, or your wood-carving practice is another type of quitting. The desire to quit a creative project happens. Sometimes we actually do quit. I've come to a place where I don't quit—I shelve. I've shelved *Only Drowning Men*, my other book manuscript, at least six times in the past two years. A previous version of myself would have been inclined to quit and walk away from it entirely, never to return. The project was too big, the challenges within it too mean and hairy.

That's Resistance.

So I let myself quit—for a month at a time, maybe two. But I put myself and Resistance on notice that I'll be back. I put my return on the calendar. That book has knocked me down a bunch of times by now. But I'm coming back for more.

FINISHING PROJECTS

I just mentioned Seth's book *The Dip*, which is about the inevitable dip that occurs as a light at the end of a project appears. The dip is the valley wherein we can get lost and fail to push the project over the finish line. Resistance, for most of us, is strongest as we approach the point where we type *The End*.

My advice: finish it. As fast as you can. Whether it's a business plan or a book or a song, know that you're going to have chances to go back and refine later. Get through the first iteration of the thing, from beginning to end, so that you have a full iteration to improve upon. The reality is that the job isn't done once you slap *The End* on it. We realize that the only thing ending is the fun part of the Work. The really grueling part is the Work that comes after finishing the first iteration: the refining, the editing, the fixing, and then the thankless drudgery that is trying to connect your Work to an audience.

POLISHING WORK

ALL FIRST DRAFTS ARE SHIT.

— ERNEST HEMINGWAY

There's a saying that the real work on a creative project doesn't start until the first draft, version, or iteration is done. The hard(er) part is moving the thing from rough to ready. This part is so hard because the whole time we want to be done with the thing while simultaneously worrying that once we release it into the world it's going to bomb.

This is also the stage where perfectionism harasses even the most relaxed of creatives. A piece of paper is only perfect until you put the first word on the page. But that's not going to stop me from fiddling with and tweaking what I've written until everything is just so.

SHIPPING PROJECTS

I used to think that the trick to being creative—the hard part —was actually doing the thing. For me, that meant writing the story or the book or whatever. I now understand that the hard parts are less about the actual production of the thing and more about what comes before and after. On the front end, it's hard to sit down in the first place day after day and do the Work. Then, on the back end, it's hard to release a project into the world.

What if it's terrible?

What if nobody likes it?

What if nobody even notices it?

We tend to care so much about the things we've made that releasing them into the wild becomes a frightening prospect. But out there is where creative projects need to be. Developing your shipping muscle is how you get (more) comfortable letting go of a thing you've spent so much time and energy bringing to life.

There are no guarantees that your thing will work once you put it out there.

The only guarantee is that it won't work if you don't ship it.

ONLY DROWNING MEN

IF YOU WANT TO GET IN SHAPE, IT'S NOT DIFFICULT. SPEND
AN HOUR A DAY RUNNING OR AT THE GYM FOR SIX MONTHS.
DONE! THAT'S NOT THE DIFFICULT PART.

THE HARD PART IS BECOMING THE SORT OF PERSON WHO
GOES TO THE GYM EVERY DAY.

— SETH GODIN, THE PRACTICE

I started writing a book shortly after the world shut down in March 2020 when COVID-19 emerged. It's now May 2022, and I'm still working on the book. Not *this* book. I'm writing this book, in part, to avoid needing to finish that book. You are indeed partaking in my literary sidepiece, so to speak.

That book is titled *Only Drowning Men*, and it's something of a memoir about my friendship with Kevin Lamb, an immensely talented writer and a good friend of mine. He was, however, as troubled and tormented as he was talented, and his life ended prematurely (by most measures) when he fell off a building in Belgrade in the fall of 2018. My book is largely a collection of emails Kevin and I exchanged between 2014 and August 2018, when I advised him to go to Serbia as a way to extend his stay in Europe.

I will finish that book, but I'm telling you about it in this book because I'm writing this book for both the characters (however nonfiction-like they both are) of that one. This is a book about the power, the potential, and the necessity of creativity.

Kevin had tremendous creative potential and drive but refused to—or was unable to—rein his impulses in enough to ever capitalize on his talent and opportunity. He had ample ideas. He spent years honing his craft both as a writer and as a performer.

He was charismatic, brave, and generous. He is also dead, I believe, largely because he lost his battle against Resistance, which we'll get into shortly.

I, on the other hand, am still writing my history in real time. The jury remains out on how well I did with the hand I've been dealt.

And you, you're in the same boat as me, I imagine.

You have creative potential. You have dreams. You have some talent.

Hopefully you've managed to make some progress on realizing your dreams. But maybe not. Either way, this little book will make the case that it is in your best interest to get to work, creatively speaking.

Leaning into creativity will lead to being a healthier, happier, fuller version of yourself. With a good deal of elbow grease and a little bit of luck, it might also lead to some professional and financial success. At the very least, it'll hopefully keep you from meeting an end like Kevin's.

GETTING OFF THE CREATIVE COUCH

As we've already discussed, you've got a fight scheduled. For today, actually. It might already be over.

And you've got another one tomorrow. Resistance is waiting for you, scheming up some devious new ways to trip you up on the way to doing your Work.

The washer might break.

The kid might break a toe.

There might be a fire at work, real or imagined.

And if you work at a place where people running around with their hair on fire is the norm, those fires might explode into full-blown conflagrations.

Plus, Resistance will always have its go-to moves to fall back on, just like the experienced boxer who knows that his right hook or her left jab is the bread and butter.

So the procrastination, the distraction, the busyness, the drama.

We train today to be better prepared to handle the match tomorrow.

Here's what our training looks like.

If you're straight off that proverbial couch, a Creative Couch Potato, then you very well might not have any idea or sense of what your Work looks like. In 2021, I hoped to run my first fifty-mile race in a forest of Ontario. But I ended up overdoing it in training, hurting my knee and sidelining me from running for a month. I really took to the more sedentary lifestyle, added some routine snacking (white cheddar popcorn mostly) during an hour or two of Netflix nightly. By the time I was healed, I didn't really want to get off the couch. And when I tried to get out for a run, I was slow, and my body didn't feel right. Not like I was still hurt, I just couldn't get into the flow of a run. The not feeling right played with my mind. Maybe I didn't feel right because I shouldn't be running.

Even as a fairly experienced runner, it was easy to fall into bad habits, and Resistance loved it.

All that to say, if you're somebody who hasn't really been doing any creative work—much less your Work—then we're going to want to get out for some creative walks before we start trying to creatively run.

You got me?

THE SIMPLICITY
OF CREATIVITY

Once we have some of our creative mojo and are lucky (or unlucky) enough to have some idea of what our Work is—unlucky because once we have something, there's immediately a pressure to then go and do it—the trick becomes improving the creative process:

- When we do our Work;
- Where we do our Work; and
- How.

If that sounds overly simplistic, it's because doing creative Work is not rocket science. Resistance wants us to believe that every day is a mountain to climb.

But most days, the challenge to doing Work isn't mountain climbing.

It's simply about putting the butt in the seat.

We make it harder on ourselves than it needs to be.

A NOTE ON MEDIUMS

You might have noticed that I haven't said much about specific mediums. There are a few reasons for that.

1. I don't want this to be a long book, and that's a deep rabbit hole.
2. I'm not qualified to write about many mediums and, quite frankly, have neither the time nor the inclination to do the work required to write those sections based on interviews.
3. The medium doesn't really matter.

Whether you're a painter or a writer or a graphic designer, an entrepreneur or a musician or a sculptor, getting in shape creatively as I'm laying it out in this book looks pretty much the same.

I believe that the battle to make Work, regardless of medium, boils down to winning that daily battle against Resistance. Once we can reliably show up ready for wrestling that rascal, the Work itself gets— wouldn't say *easy*, but—easier. It's almost like Work is the natural result or byproduct of winning the battle against Resistance. There's a Buddhist idea that sight is what naturally occurs when the eye is uncovered. Smell is the natural result of the nose being unobstructed.

When we clear Resistance from our way, the natural result is our Work.

WHERE DO YOU WORK?

According to Currey in *Daily Rituals*, Jane Austen apparently wrote in the sitting room of the family home she shared with her mother and sister and a couple other household members. The room was at the center of the house, and there were frequently people passing back and forth through it. It had a squeaky door, and Jane insisted the squeak remain so that she could hear when someone entered the room. Because, despite working on novels that would make her one of the world's most popular authors, and doing so without a private space in which to write, Jane didn't want people to know she was a writer. Only her closest family members knew.

Isaac Asimov had a little apartment in New York City where he wrote every day, all day. He was prolific, finishing more than four hundred books thanks to an incredible schedule of typing ten hours a day. Nobody else came to that apartment. It was not his home, and he did not entertain there. During an interview about his working habits, he showed the writer where he had written daily for many years. It was a desk facing a window.

Isaac pulled back the curtain back from the window with a flourish to reveal the view—a brick wall.

To do his Work, Isaac wanted—and was able to get—silence and solitude, an environment free from distractions.

Which of those two situations appeals to you more in doing your own Work?

As a younger man, I actually would have preferred the Austen setup, but in a coffee shop. I did most of my writing in my late twenties and early thirties in coffee shops, getting up regularly to get another cup of coffee, chatting with people passing through, enjoying the general din and background music. When I wrote, I felt like I was making something happen, and I wanted to be in a place where things were happening.

I've swung hard in the other direction as I approach my fortieth birthday. Maybe it's due partly to maturing. It's certainly due in part to becoming a family man. Some of it probably is due to realizing how easily distractible I am, a development that's led me to explore whether I'm actually ADHD (which would make sense but is a conversation for another book).

When we moved to a property in the forest north of Toronto, my wife and I knew we wanted to make a little space for getting creative Work done. We had visions (delusions?) of building a little cabin from scratch. I'd gone so far as to begin collecting tools and reading books about woodworking a few months earlier. Ultimately, we did get our space. The property had a new garage for 4-wheelers, a little ten-by-ten-foot room with a garage door on it. With the help of Gavin, our carpenter next-door neighbor, we converted the garage to a shed office. Sawil and I did the interior work, including lining the walls, floors, and ceiling with furniture-grade plywood. Added a few windows and a door, and voila.

It's a serene space where the sunlight throughout the day pulls different colors out of the wood and creates different feelings. It's a brilliant place to write.

Naturally, I've written zero words of this book from that shed. I'm still typing from the front seat of the Subaru, laptop on my lap. But now I'm actually just down the road from said shed, looking out over Mary Lake, several tree-covered islands rising from the waters like humongous sleeping turtles.

All this to say, we don't need a perfect writing shed to get our writing done. It might not even be a good thing. What I've found for myself and the creatives I work with isn't so much that you have a designated place for doing Work but that you have a clear idea of where you intend to Work this week, or today, at least.

Claiming the dining room table as the place where you work is just fine.

WHEN DO YOU WORK?

Historically, the biggest challenge for me sitting down to do my Work is time. Feeling like I don't have the time for that Work, which sometimes feels superfluous or not as important as other things. Feeling like I might be able to manage ten minutes, but what's the point? Feeling that to be taken seriously or have a shot as a creative, I need to spend three hours at a clip hunched over my Work.

I'm guessing you know something about those feelings. Busyness is most definitely one of Resistance's favorite ways to mess with my head. I start the morning thinking about thirty things I need to do today, and the impulse is to jump in on the to-do list right after brushing my teeth and checking my phone. Resistance knows that the longer it can keep me from sitting down through a day, the better chance it's going to win that day. By the time I get to 7 p.m., if I haven't done the Work already, there's very little chance I'm going to. By then, I'm much more likely to tip my cap to Resistance and say, "Tomorrow's another day."

My sister Christie is similar in how she works. She told me, "I like to write first thing in the morning, before other things clutter up my day." She also told me an anecdote about the poet Mary Oliver, who worked many years at a day job. She would start her day at 5 a.m., and the day would begin with writing poetry. "That way," she said, "I'll have had my say" by the time she arrived to her job.

The flip side to our early bird is the person who likes to write at night, after things have calmed down and others gone to sleep. We've already mentioned Flaubert, who wrote *Madame Bovary* under those conditions. Kafka was another writer who waited until the city slept to do his Work.

The point is, it doesn't really matter whether you Work in the morning, noontime, or night. What matters is that you clarify, carve out, claim, and protect whatever chunk of time in your day is going to be set aside for moving the Work forward. I take my own schedule week by week, mapping out which days I'm going to Work, and when during those days I intend to knock the Work out.

It doesn't need to be three hours of time, which is obvious, right? You can make a lot of ruckus creatively giving it thirty minutes a day, five days a week. String together a few weeks like that and you're getting some momentum and a pile of Work.

Does a half hour sound like too much to commit to?

How about ten minutes a day, three days a week. Can you find that?

Remember, we're talking about creative muscles here. When we're starting out as runners, the first workouts aren't marathons. The first workout is more like covering a mile in less than twenty minutes. Go do that, and then we'll talk about what comes next.

Just about everybody can cover a mile in twenty minutes, one way or another. Doing that provides the baseline from which to start building up the strength and the habit, the muscle memory that tells you: I am the sort of person who does this sort of thing. After that first mile workout, you can start to experiment with distance, with speed, with time spent on your feet. All these different throttles can be adjusted to help you make progress toward becoming a better runner, a healthier person.

The same goes for your creative Work. You'll become a better creative and a healthier, fuller version of yourself by getting more creatively fit. And when starting out, getting creatively fit means showing up today and taking one step in the direction toward creative fitness.

Becoming a Contender takes time. It requires a lot of reps over weeks, months, years. But you don't need to do years' worth of Work today. If you've got five minutes today, at'll do.

A WORD ON DISCIPLINE

DISCIPLINE = FREEDOM

—JOCKO WILLINK

In the years since giving up alcohol, I've become increasingly interested in discipline. I'm convinced that my interest in discipline is a direct response to the fact that I'm one of the least disciplined people you will ever meet. Discipline has occupied so much of my time and energy during the last decade precisely because I lack it, much the way a person thirsty in the desert can think of nothing but water.

The conventional wisdom around creativity seems to suggest that creativity is the opposite of discipline, that discipline squashes, snuffs out, inhibits, hinders, or altogether stops creativity. This view, to whatever extent it is held by anyone, is both wrong and harmful. Creativity without constraints looks more like chaos. And chaos leads to damage and destruction.

Discipline is the ability to exercise command over one's time, attention, and behavior.

I spent my twenties not writing, not creating, jumping through educational hoops, and checking off résumé boxes. I had creative ideas and dreams but mistakenly believed that creative expression was a product of inspiration, that I should wait for inspiration to compel me to sit down and type. I had it backward.

What I should have been doing, if I wanted to be making creative work, was learning discipline.

Had I improved my discipline in my twenties, I could have spent more time sitting and writing. Had I spent more time doing that, I would have produced more of a body of written work.

Why?

Because a body of written work is produced not by inspiration but by sitting and typing.

And sitting and typing is a product of discipline.

Discipline remains an alien concept to me. I really need to work at it, and I will gravitate toward chaos any chance I get.

But to get my Work done, I have to be creatively fit.

To be creatively fit, I have to work out my creative muscles daily.

And to show up for my daily creative workouts, I need discipline.

CONTENDING VIA IRISH MYTHOLOGY

Annie loved writing. She also loved Ireland, having spent three years living in Galway.

So, once she was settled back into her hometown in the midwestern United States, she began combining the two loves, writing stories about Ireland. Her stories began stretching into fantasy YA novels that she'd write around her day job in marketing.

At this point, Annie has had several books published, including the Hearts Out of Water series. USA Today took notice of those books, declaring the first book, *All The Tales We Tell*, "a darkly romantic beginning to what promises to be an unusual contemporary YA fantasy series."

She collected and connected her own set of dots.

Irish Mythology +
Writing +
Experience Growing Up as a Woman

The result is a solid body of early Work laying the groundwork for Annie's career as an author.

CONTENDING VIA ESL COPYWRITING

Nick was an English teacher by trade from the other side of the Pond, hailing from Bristol in England. Nick came to a professional crossroads and found himself needing a way to capitalize on his skills.

He experimented.

He got an idea after watching the Irish UFC fighter Conor McGregor mercilessly trash talk a Brazilian who didn't speak much English during a pre-bout press conference:

ESL Trash Talking for Cage Fighters.

If Nick had his way, when a quick-witted Irishman tried to gain the upper hand before the fight, his opponent would be able to counter with more than a punch. Nick reached out to MMA fighters over Instagram and managed to book a few calls with fighters interested in the offering.

Now, this idea was, on its face, never going to work, in that it would seemingly require teaching English to said cage fighters. For Nick to only provide his clients with catchphrases or one-liners would inevitably set them up for potentially catastrophic failure, the verbal equivalent of leaning into Conor with one's chin.

But that's neither here nor there, as that idea never gained traction.

It did, however, lead Nick to consider other applications for his writing skills in an ESL context. He next started targeting journalists to help them improve their English writing. It's another idea with some potential, but it didn't work.

Which brought Nick to a third idea.

Today he runs a business teaching English copywriting to copywriters who are not native speakers of the Queen's English. He has a sizable following on social media, posts daily tips and lessons for ESL copywriters, and has progressed from working in solely a one-on-one context to signing contracts with foreign marketing agencies.

Again, Nick collected and connected some dots:

His Copywriting Skills +
A Thing in Demand with ESL People (Copywriters) +
Social Media

CONTENDING VIA A CYA BOOK FOR ADULTS

Christie wanted to write books from an early age. She wrote stories for her family members. In high school, she wrote for the school newspaper and more stories in English classes. In college she took a turn with her writing, majoring in communications to signal a level of seriousness.

In 2014, she quit a job with a prestigious nonprofit in Washington, D.C., to travel for six months. During that time, she also rekindled her love of writing.

In 2020, she completed and published her first book, You Make the Path by Walking. It was a choose-your-own-adventure (CYA) book for restless millennials, as she described it.

Here are some dots connected to create it:
- Writing chops
- Desire to author a book
- Memory of CYA books from the 1990s
- Her experiences working and traveling around the world.

Since finishing that first book, Christie has gone on to write three other manuscripts while working full-time. Her second book will be published in 2023.

And I expect the third will be in 2024, at which point my sister will be well on her way to a second career as an author.

CREATING UNIVERSES

In the beginning, there was nothing. Vast, unfathomable expanses of freezing, airless nothingness.

And now here we are.

Our arriving here is indeed a most creative act. Whether or not there's a hand behind the process is a question for another book. For now, let's think about what the universe needed for our planet and life and multi-celled life and animals and humans and you and me to happen.

The creation of universes requires space, time, and energy.

The creation of your Work requires the same.

The space we need is both literal and mental.

Without time, we simply can't move anything forward. And as with the cosmos, creation can sometimes require a long time.

Energy is the fuel in the engine that propels us toward the goal. Get enough to eat. Get enough sleep.

As I've mentioned elsewhere, this book's creation occurred almost exclusively before 6:30 a.m., since that's when I have:

Space: Nobody's emailing me yet, the kids are still sleeping (usually), and I can duck into the shed.

Time: Carving out 45 minutes before the day starts is doable. If I don't get it done before the day gets rolling, I don't like my chances of doing it at all.

Energy: If I save the writing for the end of the day, I can almost guarantee that I lack the mental energy to do it effectively. Writing requires the high-octane fuel.

Our creative Work does indeed give us the chance to create our own little worlds.

Proceed accordingly.

COLLECTING AND CONNECTING DOTS

You could have been Annie.

You could have been Nick.

Hell, you could have done what I've done.

The dots that we've collected through observation and experience were there for the picking. None of these examples involve futuristic technology or virtuoso levels of skill in a particular discipline.

What these creative people are doing is simply connecting the dots of their lives and what they see in the world in different ways. The process of connecting those dots produces Work. Those dots lead to other dots, which lead to more Work.

So while I say that you could have done what I've done, you also couldn't have done what I've done, right?

The dots I've collected are, while not unique in and of themselves, unique to my own experience. And the way I connect them will end up looking different from how other people connect them.

As Christopher Sellers, my friend and fellow student of creativity, says, you could give five different architects the same basic set of instructions for designing a house, and you would end up with five different designs. Each architect brings their own experience and history to the process, and the final results will reflect the variety of experiences.

If you're early on in your journey as a creative (and aren't we all), know this:

You have dots to collect.

You have the ability to connect them.

Do it. Do the Work of connecting the dots you see in the world. If you can manage to defeat Resistance with some consistency, show up and put in the time, you *will* see progress. Work will get made, and you will begin to see patterns in what you do.

Fleshing out those patterns and following those paths can lead you to becoming the creative that only you can be. And in the Connection Economy, that's a ticket to both professional success and personal success.

ARRIVAL

How will you know if you've arrived at Creative Contender status? At what point can you call yourself a Contender?

I'm not precisely sure where that line is–it's different for each of us–but have a pretty good idea as to where it falls.

You're a Creative Contender when you've got two things going for you: A Body of Work and the Attitude.

A Body of Work

You don't need to have published a bunch of books or gotten your own gallery show. You do need to have shown up enough over a period of time that you start collecting different shipped projects that you can point to and say, "I made that."

It's the Body of Work that allows us to stake a claim to our corner of the Internet and prove that we belong. And the reality of our situation is that the Body of Work will (almost) always precede professional or financial success or recognition.

Attitude

Pressfield shares a story in *The War of Art* about finishing his first novel. He was living in the woods in California, doing nothing but eating, sleeping, and banging away on his old typewriter. He typed "The End" on a novel, the first he'd ever completed, one that would never find a publisher. He went down the road to tell a friend of his, a more experienced writer. "Great," the friend said, "now start on the next one today."

That's the Contender's Attitude.

I'm not saying don't celebrate the wins or don't rest. You don't need to be a workaholic to be a Contender. I'm all about celebrating the wins and taking long, luxurious breaks.

The attitude is understanding that a creative life is about Doing. The. Work. The milestones along the way are all well and good, but they're just that—milestones. Markers breaking up the time. But the progress gets made between the markers. The good stuff happens only because of what we do along the way.

The Creative Contender knows that we never actually make it to the finish line because there is no finish line. There is no winner.

There is only you.

And time.

And the blank page.

What are you going to do with that page?

Tell me:

What will you do, make, or become with your one wild and precious life?

You'll find your answer to that question in the Creative Arena.

READING LIST

A large number of books contributed to this one. Here's the best list I can come up with, in case you're interested in following me down any rabbit holes.

The War of Art and *Turning Pro* by Steven Pressfield

Big Magic by Liz Gilbert

Steal Like an Artist by Austin Kleon

The Dip and *Tribes* by Seth Godin

Daily Rituals by Mason Currey

ACKNOWLEDGMENTS

I heard an episode of her Big Magic podcast where Liz Gilbert was talking about how the first book is always easier to write than the second. The first book had been baking for twenty years before the writer ever put their butt in the seat.

This book is twenty years in the making.

I've got a lot of people to thank.

To Christie, my sister and chief partner in crimes against conformity, I wouldn't have written this book without your support.

Sawil, this book (and the life I'm loving living) would not have happened without you.

To Mom and Dad and Michelle, thank you for the sacrifices, guidance, and love.

Sara, your support in getting this thing over the finish line was invaluable, even if I do object to the CMS approach to numbers. Evan, for snapping design victory from the jaws of defeat, I'm in your debt.

I want to thank the Rowdies who supported me during the Rowdy Sprints when I was writing this book. You helped keep my chin up and the load light.

Finally, thanks to everybody on LinkedIn who chimed in along the way as I shared about this process in public.

ABOUT THE AUTHOR

Tony Albrecht is a writer, social entrepreneur, and student of the creative process. Tony co-founded The Rowdy Creative and The Wilds & The Woods, and he works with people old enough to know they want a different trajectory and young and crazy enough to believe that big change is possible. His work is informed by his recovery from two afflictions, alcoholism and becoming a lawyer.

Tony lives in a forest in Ontario, Canada, with his wife and two children, who both insist on growing up too fast.

Made in the USA
Monee, IL
12 September 2022

13834655R00073